Courage

Kimberley Jane Pryor

Marshall Cavendish
Benchmark
New York

This edition first published in 2009 in the United States of America by Marshall Cavendish Benchmark.

Marshall Cavendish Benchmark
99 White Plains Road
Tarrytown, NY 10591
www.marshallcavendish.us

First published in 2008 by
MACMILLAN EDUCATION AUSTRALIA PTY LTD
15–19 Claremont St, South Yarra 3141

Visit our Web site at www.macmillan.com.au or go directly to www.macmillanlibrary.com.au

Associated companies and representatives throughout the world.

Library of Congress Cataloging-in-Publication Data

Pryor, Kimberley Jane.
    Courage / by Kimberley Jane Pryor.
        p. cm. — (Values)
    Includes index.
    ISBN 978-0-7614-3131-2
    1. Courage—Juvenile literature. 2. Children—Conduct of life—Juvenile literature. I. Title.
    BJ1533.C8P79 2008
179'.6—dc22

                                            2008001662

Edited by Helena Newton
Text and cover design by Christine Deering
Page layout by Raul Diche and Domenic Lauricella
Photo research by Naomi Parker and Legend Images

Printed in the United States

Acknowledgments

The author and the publisher are grateful to the following for permission to reproduce copyright material:

Front cover photograph of friends building a birdhouse courtesy of Photos.com

Photos courtesy of:
BananaStock, 20; BrandX Pictures, 8; Corbis RF, 30; Blend Images/Getty Images, 14, 28; Digital Archive Japan, INC./Getty Images, 27; Digital Vision/Getty Images, 15; © Griselda Amorim/iStockphoto.com, 24; © Galina Barskaya/iStockphoto.com, 26; © Chris Bernard/iStockphoto.com, 7; © Michael Braun/iStockphoto.com, 17; © Jennifer Daley/iStockphoto.com, 18; © Elena Elisseeva/iStockphoto.com, 22; © Greg Ferguson/iStockphoto.com, 23; © Juliana Halvorson/iStockphoto.com, 13; © Eileen Hart/iStockphoto.com, 4; © bonnie jacobs/iStockphoto.com, 19; © Nancy Louie/iStockphoto.com, 6; © mandygodbehear/iStockphoto.com, 25; © marmion/iStockphoto.com, 3, 29; © Carmen Mart/iStockphoto.com, 9; © MidwestWilderness/iStockphoto.com, 10; © Brad Sauter/iStockphoto.com, 11; © sonyae/iStockphoto.com, 12; Photos.com, 1, 5, 16, 21.

While every care has been taken to trace and acknowledge copyright, the publisher tenders their apologies for any accidental infringement where copyright has proved untraceable. Where the attempt has been unsuccessful, the publisher welcomes information that would redress the situation.

For Nick, Ashley and Thomas

1 3 5 6 4 2

Contents

Glossary words
When a word is printed in **bold**, you can look up its meaning in the Glossary on page 31.

Values

Values are the things you believe in. They guide the way:

- you think
- you speak
- you **behave**

Values help you to play fairly with friends on a swing.

4

Values help you to decide what is right and what is wrong. They also help you to live your life in a **meaningful** way.

Values help you to follow the rules of a clapping game.

Courage

Courage is being brave and trying new things. It is **participating** in activities that might seem scary at first.

You participate when you say something in a class discussion.

Courage is also **attempting** to do something you want to be able to do. It is trying to make something you want to be able to make.

If you want to make paper airplanes that fly well, give it a try.

People who Show Courage

People who show courage keep trying because they want to **succeed**. They do not give up if they make a mistake.

People who want to be good at kicking a ball keep practicing.

People who have courage also like to visit new places. They have fun with their family, friends, and neighbors.

When you visit a petting zoo, you can try feeding the animals even if you're a bit frightened.

Trying New Things with Family

Families can show courage by trying new things together. Sometimes families go to new places for vacations or try new activities on the weekends.

Going hiking together is one way families try new things.

You may like to try some of the activities that other family members enjoy. You might find that you enjoy these activities too.

Family members can enjoy riding bodyboards together.

Trying New Things with Friends

Trying new things with friends helps you to **discover** something different. You can share good music and funny books.

You may find that you and your friends like reading the same books.

A friend might ask you to go somewhere you have never been before. You may find that you enjoy a new place that seems scary at first.

Friends might ask you to try the rides at a new park.

Trying New Things with Neighbors

Sometimes neighbors get together to try something new. They share ideas and **skills**.

Neighbors sometimes go to craft classes together.

Many neighbors take part in "Earth Day" activities together. They clean up and protect their local environment by removing garbage and planting trees.

Neighbors often join in and work together on "Earth Day."

Ways To Show Courage

There are many different ways to show courage toward your family, friends, and neighbors. Participating is a good way to show courage.

Making a birdhouse with a friend can be fun.

Trying new things and doing your best are also good ways to show courage. Being brave is another way to show courage.

It takes courage to go on a roller coaster.

Participating

Participating is one way to show courage. When you participate, you find out which sports and activities you enjoy.

People of all ages enjoy flying kites.

There are many ways to participate at school. Trying out for the school play or a sports team are fun ways to take part.

Participating in the school play is a fun way to try something new.

Trying New Things

Trying new things is another way to show courage. People who show courage are not afraid to try new foods.

There may be foods at a party that you have never tried before.

20

Trying new things can be scary. It may be better to do something for a short while the first time you try it.

You may feel nervous the first time you swim in your neighbor's pool.

Doing Your Best

Doing your best means trying as hard as you can to do something well. You do not know how well you can do something until you try.

You may be able to turn a good cartwheel if you try hard.

It is more important to do your **personal best** than to win a race. Your personal best is the best you have ever done in that kind of race.

Achieving a personal best at a sports event is a great feeling.

Being Brave

People who have courage are brave. Being brave is having the strength to do something that seems a bit frightening.

It is brave to let a bird sit on your shoulder.

You are being brave when you stand up to bullies. It is also brave to stand up for friends who are being bullied.

Bullies can make others feel angry or sad.

Not Giving Up Easily

Not giving up easily is part of showing courage. It takes a lot of time and **effort** to learn something new.

You will learn to do more skateboard tricks if you do not give up easily.

People who do not give up easily eventually learn new skills. They find out that they can be good at many different things.

If you practice playing the piano, your playing will improve.

Learning from Mistakes

People who have courage learn from their mistakes. When they make a mistake, they ask themselves, "What should I do differently next time?"

People who fall on cement learn that it is safer to play on grass.

Knowing that it is okay to make mistakes is part of having courage. Everyone makes mistakes sometimes.

Teachers help students if they make mistakes when they first learn to read.

Personal Set of Values

There are many different values. Everyone has a personal set of values. This set of values guides people in big and little ways in their daily lives.

If you are training to become a hurdler, you need to have the courage to try.

Glossary

attempting   trying

behave   act in a certain way

discover   find something new

effort   hard work

meaningful   important ot valuable

participating   taking part

personal best   the best someone has ever done in a
particular type of race

skills   abilities that help you to do activities
or jobs well

succeed   do something well

Index